PIECES OF A PUZZLE

By: Bevlique Garrett

Dedication:

This Book is dedicated to my mother Rosalind Nicole Ward. Without her strength, prayers, resilience and guidance I don't know where I would be! I can only hope something in my writings contributes to the world's growth, as she has mine.

To the reader:

Thank You for purchasing my first book of poetry! Welcome to a jumbo of my 35 year journey on this earth. These poems reflect the space I now operate from. I sincerely hope each and every growing soul can appreciate and take from my humble expressions. It is my intention to ignite that spark of change while spreading light through this gift.

                              Wellness and Balanced Vibrations

Contents

Unititled	4
Who has awaken this pen	5
Crazy Love Song	6
Untitled	7
11 Seconds	8
Jazz	9
S.G.O	10
Untitled	11
G	12
Big Apple	13
The Present	14
Rain	15
Ain't that some shit	16
Zombies	17
Stormy Weather	18
Sleeping Giants	19
Tales of blessed souls	20
Unititled	21
Peace	22
Love	23
Free	24
A place	25
New Day	26

Untitled

The sky is open…

Vast and Free

Swift breeze,

Like sunshine on earth's face,

Time does not exist here,

Past never present….

A Gift,

Wise ones value this,

Meanwhile intimate conversations with Sirius,

Analysis of centuries,

Not many get as high as me,

Wanna elevate to Divine Royalty???

Find yourself a Queen!

Lol…

Who has awaken this pen?

Who has awaken this pen?

It has startled me...

Sent jolts through every major artery,

...It consumes me-seeps deep into my DNA,

Finds my right hand and displays its soul

Everything laid out to the open sea,

Who has awaken this pen?

It cares nothing of time or priorities,

Only the message inside of me,

That is it's one and only concern,

As it Lives within I learn,

Not to run not to hide,

To see beneath the lies-

Besides "Vision is always better through the 3rd eye",

I smiled sat and thought...

Then replied...

"You're right! Peace be unto you Oh Divine Light!"

Who has awaken this pen?

Crazy Love Song

An irresistible melody...

Relentlessly haunting the beat of my heart,

Ironically- I hum along....

Crazy Love Song

Untitled

When the cocoon breaks,

Recreation emerges...

The Next Level of elevation,

Another ayah in the structure,

A chapter closed in the story of evolution...

The hearts only true desire- Freedom 2 Grow!

11 secs

No Time is present here,

This moment has only grown!

Oh what little say so we have...

When the heart decides,

It will rise in the most turbulent of waters,

Wrestle the savage beast trapped in human beings,

Journey through hot sand and cold mountains...

11yrs in this war...

My hearts decision **STANDS**,

As if it were the 1st 11 seconds all over again...

JAZZ

The Atmosphere of peace,

Joy basking in serenity,

Heartbreak a faint echo...

Love – Lives- "Hear?"

In every cord, note, string and horn,

The Pulse-The Drum,

Free Rhythm...

Creating symphonies-Ecstasy to the soul,

The way those keys sing topsy

In Howard Rumsey's light house All – Stars...

Maybe Miles and John are up to something again...

Heavenly that is...

Mr. Parker can sure blow...

Like a summer breeze,

Accompanied by warm sunshine...

I'm talkin' Jazz mannnn...

JAZZ!

S.G.O in progress

A new genesis,

With each sunrise,

"I will do a new thing in you"

Says the light,

There is no drug in existence,

That could allow one to experience

Such internal and eternal bliss,

A Spiritual Growth Overdose...Never KILLED Nobody!

Untitled

A still moment,

Clarity and peace...

Giving calm to inner turmoil,

Forcing all in its presence to balance,

Healing melodies dressed in morning sunshine...

How great thou art! Oh Divine!

<u>G</u>

What is that thing in you that doesn't quit-won't give up!

Buried deep yet penetrating every surface,

An inner beast,

Feasting on adversity,

Turning obstacles into opportunities,

I know that's – that "G" in me,

When you look in the mirror,

See it in you!

Big Apple

That brisk air, the smell... (Slow deep breathe)

No sleep in the city,

That sound never ends,

Trains, Taxis, buses, people, transactions

Things are happening everywhere!

All to a rhythm of its own,

If you got the heart- when you see it,

Succulent, Red, Hot, sweet in every spot,

Take a bite...of that Big Apple!

The Present

Each day a gift,

Will you open it?

Appreciate and be grateful for its contents,

Every hour unwrapped,

Every minute a new opportunity,

Every second a new birth...

Expansion of mind and soul,

Spiritual elevation through evolution,

Choosing consciously in every moment to vibrate higher,

Each day a gift,

Will you open it?

The present (BE)

Rain

Rain!

We hate to get wet,

It's uncomfortable,

If it's cold you mustn't be out too long you could get sick or that chill will start to bite,

Not very cozy or warm...

Yet necessary...

If it didn't rain you would beg the sky for hydration, something to cool the summer sun's blaze, water the crops, plants, trees

After all seeds don't grow without water,

Right?

Rain!

We hate to get wet,

It's uncomfortable,

Yet essential to growth!

Ain't that some shit!

Many Lessons although at times teachers wear disguises,

The worst times of life,

Yet the wisdom gained is essential,

To your evolution-spiritual and psychological elevation,

Now ain't that some shit!

Zombies

...Sshh

You hear that?

Stillness ushers in silence,

Peace the language of divinity,

Those who are familiar with such surroundings create beautiful

Expressions of freedom,

Those who aren't familiar with such surroundings create painful expressions,

Of a desire or need,

Are you living or just breathing?

A planet of people wrapped in false securities,

Lost touch and essence,

Souls that scramble to feel something deeper,

Searching the world for what lies inside...

Stormy weather

It's never 100% smooth sailing,

 Winds come and go,

Rain falls – thunder roars,

Lightning flashes that illuminate the night,

Sometimes all at the same time...

The boat swayed they awaken Christ,

Hearing of their fear he replies,

"Oh ye of little faith"...

There is a living presence to usher you through the storm,

How great it is to see the sunshine, hear the birds sing, see flowers bloom...

After the storm!

Sleeping Giants

Journey...

What has come to be cannot without it,

Many a soul knows only choices of fear,

Sleeping giants drowning in puddles,

As radiance from the sun brings warmth and light,

Awaken- standing up,

Puddles at its feet barely rising over its massive toes,

One giant laughs at his folly...

Echoes disturb the others

Who now stand in illumination with water at their feet,

They Begin to plant the seeds of a new eternity

Tales of blessed souls

Blessed souls tell tall tales of basking in the eternal sunshine,

Holy Communion -divine union,

What wonders come with a gentle swift breeze?

No adjectives exist that could give life to the liberation from mind,

Soaring of a heart,

Unlimited potential unveiled,

Nature's brilliant symphonies usher me outside this illusion we call day to day life,

With a long deep breathe comes renewal,

Perspective change,

Nothing soothes like warm rays from the brightest star,

The slightest movement sends ripples throughout waters...

As thoughts and vibrational frequencies we emit into our universe,

When you speak of life hopefully this description is close,

If not perhaps you should try living first!

Untitled

If nothing is truly impossible...

Our limitations lie in our fears,

Cozy, warm, comfortable, stubborn and

Woven into the fiber of your being since conception,

Oh what chains to break...?

The renewing of that mind is true resurrection,

As with each days sunrise,

Startled and stumbling, drowsy from such deep sleeps,

Oh ye weary souls keep walking on more will join you- soon your legs

Will become strong,

The fog will fade- a new world opens up,

Embraces you,

Look not to the clouds for a man,

Instead awaken the Christ inside you!

<u>Peace</u>

Steady knocking almost to a beat,

It echoes...

Yet no answer,

No one lives there anymore,

That gloomy cage of fear, anger, unrest,

This place has been deserted,

Packed what I could carry on my back,

Built a raft,

Drifted far out into sea,

Completely unknown to modern geography,

Yet a seagull whispered its name quietly...

Peace...

LOVE

I am love...

Therefor certain of it,

Having peaked in the doors of compassion,

Companionship with my soul an essential,

A longing arises within-desire has been tamed,

Soul in full bloom...

The morning dew from yesterday evenings spring joins

Nights chill providing moisture,

In the stillness of days first light,

I am embraced by long arms of the sun coming just over that horizon,

A gentle wind speaks eloquently,

Birds, bees, stars, tall trees,

Tell captivating stories of a universe inside me,

Love is...

We need not worry that it won't **BE**,

Love says simply "give of me"

Free

"Do it Bevlique!"

Put the pen on the paper...

Somethings there!

No don't think just write,

"Be water my friend" said Mr. Lee,

Allow the flow never mind its direction...

Words like birds flying

Free!

A Place

I know of a place...

Where peace is the fragrance,

Inhale and exhale that atmosphere,

Joy is not limited but wide, vast, expanding

Abundance is everywhere emanating from the depths of "being"...

Like the essence of energy eternally flowing,

Streams of stardust floating across unknown galaxies,

I know of a place...

GOD lives, breathes, manifest-

Love is the fragrance,

Now is always the time!

No limitations truth no longer relative

But absolute- Knowing Now is powerful,

Presence says I am...

I know of a place,

If you're willing to journey inside you!

New Day

Warm rays of light penetrate my bedroom window,

Gently massaging my face,

Blue skies everywhere,

Spirit consumes me with a long, deep breathe,

Happy New Day...

Made in the USA
Columbia, SC
12 April 2024

34123527R00015